SCIENCE ISSUES

Genetic engineering

Pennie Stoyles, Peter Pentland, and David Demant

This edition first published in 2004 in the United States of America by
Smart Apple Media.

Smart Apple Media
1980 Lookout Drive
North Mankato
Minnesota 56003

Library of Congress Cataloging-in-Publication Data

Stoyles, Pennie.
    Genetic engineering / by Pennie Stoyles, Peter Pentland, and David Demant.
    p. cm. — (Science issues)

    Summary: Discusses two sides of issues related to genetic engineering—whether
DNA profiling violates a person's right to privacy, whether genetically modified
foods are safe, and whether plants and animals should be cloned.

    ISBN 1-58340-330-2
    1. Genetic engineering—Juvenile literature. 2. Genetic engineering—
Social aspects—Juvenile literature. [1. Genetic engineering.] I. Pentland, Peter.
II. Demant, David. III. Title.
    QH442.S773 2003
    303.48'3—dc21   2002044624

First Edition
9 8 7 6 5 4 3 2 1

First published in 2003 by
MACMILLAN EDUCATION AUSTRALIA PTY LTD
627 Chapel Street, South Yarra, Australia 3141

Associated companies and representatives throughout the world.

Edited by Sally Woollett
Text and cover design by Polar Design Pty Ltd
Illustrations by Alan Laver, Shelly Communications
Photo research by Jes Senbergs

Printed in Thailand

Acknowledgements
The author and the publisher are grateful to the following for permission to
reproduce copyright material:

Cover photograph: Dolly the Sheep, courtesy of Derek Bromhall—OSF/Auscape.

Derek Bromhall—OSF/Auscape, p. 29; Coo-ee Picture Library, pp. 5, 25 (top); Corbis
Digital Stock, p. 9; CRC for Innovative Dairy Products, p. 27; The DW Stock Picture
Library, pp. 18 (top right), 20 (top), 20 (center), 23; Getty Images, pp. 6, 11, 15, 16,
18 (bottom), 19, 21 (bottom), 22; Jiri Lochman/Lochmann Transparencies, p. 18
(top left); Dale Mann/Retrospect, pp. 14, 21 (top); Terry Oakley/The Picture Source,
pp. 20 (bottom), 26, 30; Photolibrary.com, pp. 4, 7, 28; Reuters, p. 17; Rubberball,
p. 25 (bottom).

While every care has been taken to trace and acknowledge copyright, the publisher
tenders their apologies for any accidental infringement where copyright has proved
untraceable. Where the attempt has been unsuccessful, the publisher welcomes
information that would redress the situation.

Contents

Glossary words
When a word is printed in **bold** you can look up its meaning in the Glossary on page 31.

 Look out for these questions. Try to think about them while you read each issue in this book.

Genetic engineering

Strawberry plants grow the best and sweetest fruits in cool climates. But if the strawberries get too cold overnight and freeze solid, they are ruined.

Many fish can live in salt water that gets very cold, many degrees below the freezing point of their own bodies. This is because they contain a natural substance in their blood that prevents it from freezing—a special fish antifreeze!

So what do strawberries and fish have in common?

Scientists called **genetic engineers** have recently worked out a way to stop strawberries from freezing when they are still on the plant. They can make the strawberries produce the same antifreeze as the fish. They do this in a process called genetic engineering.

Genetics is the scientific study of how characteristics of plants and animals are **inherited**.

∨ Cells contain particular genetic codes that
∨ tell them how to grow.

Genetic engineers have worked out that the **cells** of some fish contain a particular code that instructs the cells to make antifreeze. They have transferred that code into some strawberry plants to help them to grow successfully in cold climates.

Putting fish antifreeze into strawberries is only one of the things that genetic engineers can do. Genetic engineers also:

- help to solve crimes
- genetically modify crops
- **clone** animals
- search for cures for diseases.

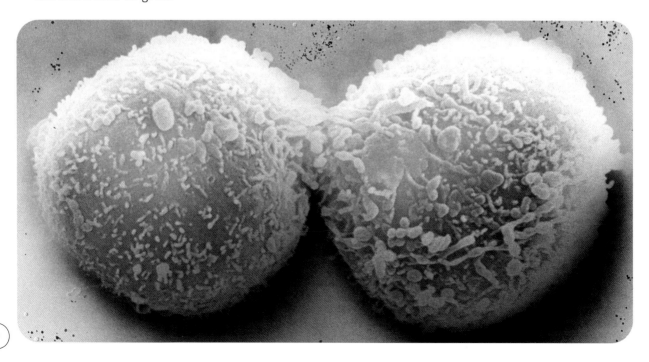

Genetic engineering is a science issue

Should antifreeze be put into strawberries to stop them being ruined in freezing temperatures?

Many people believe that the things that genetic engineers do are wrong. They believe that genetic engineering interferes with the laws of nature. Other people see genetic engineering as a great benefit in areas such as agriculture and medical science. There are also people who have not yet made up their minds. This makes genetic engineering a science issue.

Different points of view

Sometimes you have to decide what you think about something. Before you decide whether something is good or bad, or right or wrong, you usually try to find out about the subject and listen to what other people think. There may be two opposite points of view. Different people or groups may have several different views. This is what makes something an issue.

Can you trust everything you read and hear? It is a good idea to look carefully at the people who are arguing about an issue. Do they know all of the facts? Are they only giving one side of the issue because they have something to gain? You should not simply accept what people say. Think about what they say and why they say it.

^ Think about the source of your information before you accept it.

THIS BOOK will help you understand more about some genetic engineering issues. It tries to be balanced. Two sides of each issue are presented to help you to decide what *you* think.

You will:

- find out about **DNA profiling**
- find out how genetics can make people healthier
- find out why people want to ban foods that have been genetically changed
- learn about cloning and Dolly the sheep.

Understanding genetic engineering

Have you ever noticed that your friends have differently shaped noses or that some of your friends look a lot like their parents?

Your genetic code

You have a particular set of genetic characteristics that makes you unique. Unless you are an identical twin, no one else in the world has your exact set of genetic characteristics.

Most of your characteristics are inherited from your parents. In almost every cell in your body there is information that is a code for a special human—you. It is your genetic code. This code stays the same throughout your life and can be passed on to your children.

Inheritance and environment

As well as your genetic code, your environment has an effect on you. The types of foods you eat and the exercise you do will influence your health and your body shape.

^ Can you see some genetic characteristics that these parents have passed on to their children?

Your height depends on both inheritance and environment. It is inherited from your parents, but a healthy diet will also make you grow taller.

Your eye color is dependent on your inheritance. No matter what you eat, what exercises you do, or how much television you watch, they stay the same color.

<<
No matter what sort of muscles you inherit from your parents, lifting weights will make them bigger.

Chromosomes and genes

To find out more about the genetic code, you need to look inside cells. Cells are the microscopic building blocks that make all living things. You have about six billion of them making up your body!

Chromosomes

In the center of most of your cells is a part called the **nucleus**. If you use a microscope to look at the nucleus of one of your cells you can see tiny striped strands called **chromosomes**. These chromosomes contain your entire genetic code.

Humans have 46 chromosomes in almost every cell in their bodies. Chromosomes come in 23 matching pairs. One member of each pair came from your mother and the other from your father.

∨ Humans have 23 pairs of
∨ chromosomes in almost every cell.

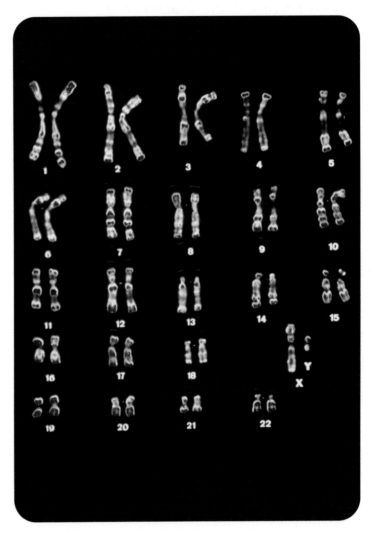

Genetic gossip

Different species of plants and animals have particular numbers of chromosomes in their cells.

Corn	20
Fruit fly	8
Gorilla	48
Lettuce	18
Horse	64

Genes

Each chromosome contains thousands of **genes**. Each gene is a code for one genetic characteristic. The genes are arranged on the chromosomes in a precise order. For example, a gene that codes for your blood type is always in the same place on the ninth pair of chromosomes in each cell.

The amazing thing about chromosomes is that each set of chromosomes in every cell in your body is identical, so every one of your cells contains all the information needed to make you who you are.

DNA

Chromosomes are made of a chemical called **d**eoxy-ribo-**n**ucleic **a**cid, or DNA for short. We know each chromosome contains thousands of genes, so a gene is just a small section of DNA. DNA is an amazing chemical because it can make exact copies of itself. So every time your body makes a new cell, a new copy of your DNA is made.

The shape and structure of DNA are what makes it special. It is called a double **helix**. The shape is like a twisted ladder. The "rungs" of the ladder are made of pairs of chemicals called bases. There are four different bases, shown by the letters A, G, C, and T. The order of the bases is what makes the genetic code.

>>
This is part of a DNA molecule. It looks like a twisted ladder. The code is in the "rungs" of the ladder.

How does DNA code for your characteristics?

The order of bases in your DNA tells your body what **proteins** to make to give you your own special characteristics. Proteins are everywhere in your body. They make up your cells and they control all the activities that go on in your body such as digestion of food, muscle movement, and even thinking.

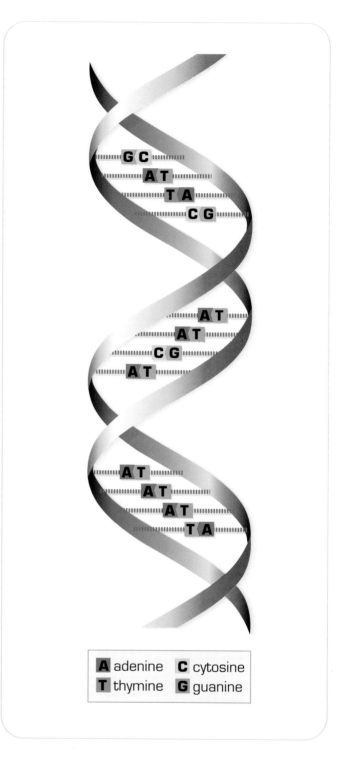

| **A** adenine | **C** cytosine |
| **T** thymine | **G** guanine |

CCACCCTTGGAGTTCACTCACCTAAACCTCAAACTAATAAAGCTTG
GTTCTTTTCTCCGACACGCAAAGGAAGCGCTAAGGTAAATGCATCA
GACCCACACTGCCGCGGAACTTTTCGGCTCTCTAAGGCTGTATTTT
GATATACGAAAGGCACATTTTCCTTCCCTTTTCAAAATGCACCTTGC
AAACGTAACAGGGACCCGACTAGGATCATCGGGAAAAGGAGGAGG

<<
This is part of a genetic code for a disease. You can see that the bases are arranged in a particular order.

How inheritance works

We know that we inherit our characteristics from both of our parents. We also know that most cells in our bodies contain 23 pairs of chromosomes. There are some cells that contain only 23 single chromosomes. These are the sex cells, called sperm cells in men and egg cells in women.

When a sperm cell and an egg cell join together, the 23 single chromosomes pair up to make a double set of coded instructions for a new person.

>>
You inherit a double set of information for each of your genetic characteristics.

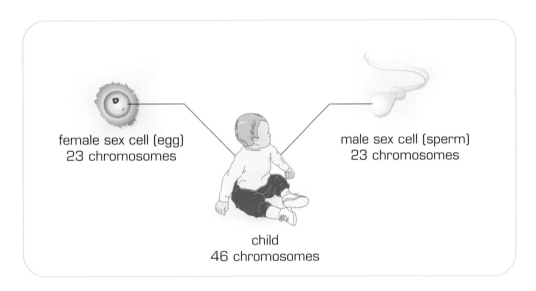

female sex cell (egg)
23 chromosomes

male sex cell (sperm)
23 chromosomes

child
46 chromosomes

Blended characteristics

Many of your genetic characteristics are a blend of both your parents' characteristics. Say, for example, that your mother has straight hair and your father has curly hair. You might inherit a "straight hair" gene from your mother, and a "curly hair" gene from your father. You will probably end up with wavy hair, halfway between curly and straight.

∨ ∨ This child has wavy hair, which is a blend of straight and curly hair.

Dominant and recessive characteristics

Not all characteristics blend together. Inheritance of eye color works differently. If you inherit a "brown eyes" gene from your mother and a "blue eyes" gene from your father, you will have brown eyes! The gene for brown eyes is "stronger" or **dominant** over the gene for blue eyes. The gene for blue eyes is in your cells but it does not show up because it is "weaker" or **recessive**.

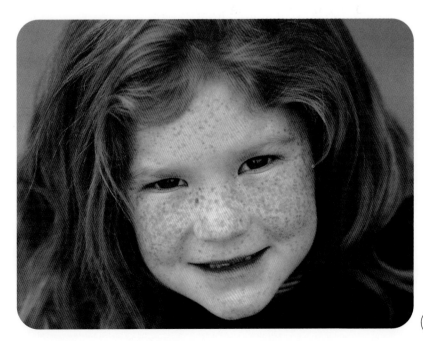

DNA profiling

The Genesville Gazette

Parent Outrage at Gene Testing of Students

Parents at Genesville School have been outraged by a move by Principal Carey to take the genetic fingerprints of every student and member of staff at the school.

The extraordinary decision has come about following the theft of a laptop computer from the principal's office early last Monday morning. Principal Carey arrived at the school at 10.30 A.M. to discover that the office door was open and the computer was missing.

Detectives investigating the crime found a freshly used tissue in the wastebasket. Detective Inspector Rex Dogsbody observed that there was enough genetic material in the tissue to make a genetic fingerprint. This was when Principal Carey ordered the testing of all staff and students.

"If they are innocent they have nothing to worry about!" said a defiant Principal Carey yesterday. "It is a simple test. All they have to do is have a few cells scraped from inside their mouths."

Parents, however, are concerned. They see it as an invasion of their children's privacy. They are also worried that the genetic information might be sold to outside organizations such as the police or insurance companies. The cost of the fingerprinting is yet another issue. Each genetic "fingerprint" costs about $300 to produce.

"We have to wonder what was on that computer," said one parent.

DNA and identity

We know that, except for identical twins, no two people have the same DNA. Genetic engineers and other scientists can identify a person by their DNA using a process called DNA profiling.

DNA contains all the information that identifies you. In your DNA there are genes that code for obvious characteristics such as hair color, eye color, and your blood type. Your DNA also contains information that is not so obvious, such as whether you are likely to go bald, or get diabetes later in life, or if you might pass on an inherited disease to your children.

What are the issues about DNA profiling?

DNA profiling can determine if you are at risk of certain medical conditions in the future. It can also be used to help solve a crime. In the newspaper story on the previous page, the principal wants the police to take DNA samples from all the staff and students. But if the police did take the DNA, they may find out other information, including things that the staff and students and their parents do not yet know. This information could be kept on the police files.

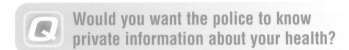

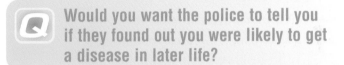

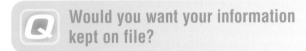

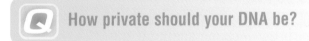

ˇ Information from your
ˇ DNA could be stored on file.

Making DNA profiles

Three things about DNA make it possible to identify people using their DNA:

- Everyone's DNA is different (except for identical twins).
- DNA is in almost every cell in our bodies.
- DNA can make exact copies of itself.

Only the tiniest sample—a single cell or even just the sweat from a fingerprint—is needed to make a DNA profile.

Genetic gossip

DNA profiling was accidentally discovered by an English man, Sir Alec Jeffreys, in 1984.

In a laboratory, the DNA sample is copied until there is enough DNA to test. The sample is cut up into differently sized pieces using chemicals called **enzymes**. The number and size of the pieces and the genetic code on each piece is different for different people.

The DNA pieces are put onto a special jelly. Electricity is passed through the jelly, which makes all the DNA pieces spread out into a pattern that looks a bit like a bar code. The DNA pattern is called a DNA profile. The DNA profile of a suspect can be compared with DNA found at a crime scene. If the positions of the bars match up, then it is likely that the samples are from the same person.

∧ Can you match the suspect to the sample?

Comparing profiles

Before DNA profiling was developed, fingerprints were used to identify people suspected of crimes because, like DNA, no two people have the same set of fingerprints. In many countries, anybody who is suspected of a crime has their fingerprints taken even before it is proved that they are guilty or innocent. The fingerprints are stored in files so that they can be compared with fingerprints found at a crime scene.

Criminals often wear gloves or wipe away their fingerprints, but they may leave hair, flakes of dead skin, or **saliva** at a crime scene. These forms of evidence can be used to make a DNA profile.

A DNA profile from a crime scene must be compared with another one to prove someone was at the crime scene. If the police have a suspect, they can take a sample of DNA from the suspect for comparison. They usually take a hair, saliva, or blood sample to get the DNA. DNA samples are sometimes taken from people in order to remove them from a list of suspects.

Genetic gossip

Did you know that you shed between 30,000 and 40,000 skin cells every minute? Skin cells make up most of the dust around your house. You also lose about 70 hairs every day.

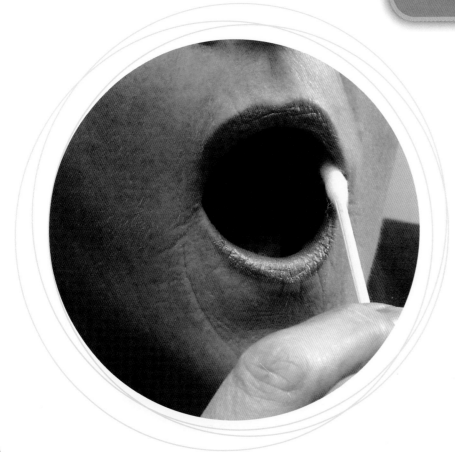

<<
This person is having a DNA sample taken. The DNA is in cheek cells that flake off into the saliva.

Profiling the population

Some people believe that everyone in the population should be DNA profiled. A huge file of everyone's DNA could be kept, and every time a crime is committed and some DNA found, the file could be checked to help solve the crime.

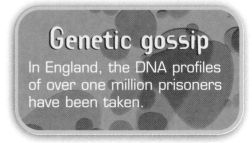

Other people believe that all criminals who are in jail should have their DNA profiled. This is because many criminals commit more than one crime.

Time and money

Making a DNA profile is much more time consuming and expensive than taking a set of fingerprints. Some people think it would be a waste of money to test everybody, especially people who have never committed crimes.

Private information

Imagine if your parents read your private diary and then told everyone what was written there! A DNA profile is a bit like a diary of all your characteristics.

Your DNA profile may show that you could go bald when you are older. It may show that you are likely to get heart disease when you are older. Would you want to know that? Would you want other people such as your employer to know that?

∨ Who should know your
∨ private information?

 # The DNA profiling debate

DNA profiling is a very useful tool. It can provide information in some medical situations and in solving crimes. It can also reveal private information about you.

Arguments against

Other people disagree with DNA profiling of the whole population because:

- [X] it will cost a lot of money
- [X] it is an invasion of personal privacy
- [X] it may tell you information about yourself that you prefer not to know
- [X] the laws will not be able to stop people from using your information.

Arguments for

Some people agree with DNA profiling of the whole population because:

- [✓] it is the only way to identify someone positively when there are no fingerprints at the scene of a crime
- [✓] it will discourage people thinking about committing crimes
- [✓] it may allow people to identify health problems at an early stage
- [✓] it may help people to avoid future health problems.

Other opinions

Other people believe that DNA profiles should only be taken from some people, such as suspects or people who have committed crimes in the past. They also think that the laws should be changed to control the use of genetic information and to protect people's privacy.

What is your opinion?

Q Who should have their DNA profile taken?

Q Should governments know the information stored in everybody's DNA?

Q What new laws about DNA profiles should there be?

<<
DNA profiles can be used in courts, but is this an invasion of privacy?

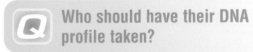

Genetic modification

Fat facts

Many people have to cut down on the amount of fat they eat because they have heart or blood pressure problems. Most fat from animals is called "saturated" fat. Another type of fat (usually from plants) is called "unsaturated" fat. Unsaturated fat is generally better for you and can help to avoid heart or blood pressure problems. People with these problems are often told by their doctor to eat less meat, butter, and cheese, which come from animals and contain saturated fats. They are advised to eat vegetable oils and nuts, which contain unsaturated fats.

According to some reports, Japanese scientists have been able to put genes from spinach plants into the DNA of hogs. The spinach gene changes the hogs' saturated fat to unsaturated fat. The genetically altered hogs contain 20 percent less saturated fat than normal hogs. This makes products such as pork and bacon healthier to eat.

∨∨ Some hogs are genetically altered with genes from spinach plants.

Genetically modified foods

Changing or modifying the genes of plants and animals in the laboratory is called genetic modification. Foods made from these plants and animals are called genetically modified (GM) foods.

Genetic modification may be used to:

- make foods healthier
- increase the yields of crops
- make crops **resistant** to pests and diseases
- make crops more resistant to chemicals used to kill weeds or other pests
- allow plants and animals to grow in a wider range of climates.

>>
These people are protesting about genetically modified foods and seeds. Some people are not yet sure if GM foods are safe to eat.

What are the issues about genetic modification?

The way that scientists make GM foods is very new. Not many people properly understand the process. When people do not understand something new, they are often afraid of it.

People are naturally careful about what they eat. They like to know that their food is healthy and safe. Many people believe that GM foods should be tested for a few more years before they are sold. Some people believe that GM foods should be banned.

Other people think the world's population is growing so quickly that we will not be able to produce enough to feed everyone. They believe that unless we make GM crops that use less land, water, and **pesticides**, there will be widespread starvation.

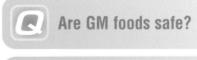
Q Are GM foods safe?

Q Is genetic modification okay if it does not involve the food we eat?

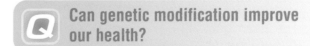
Q Can genetic modification improve our health?

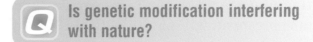
Q Is genetic modification interfering with nature?

Modifying plants and animals

Humans have been improving crops and animal herds for thousands of years. Farmers choose the healthiest animals to breed to make a new herd. They choose the strongest seeds to grow plants that produce bigger and better grains, fruits, and vegetables. They can even make new varieties by breeding closely related species together.

<< The carrot tops on the left are part of a wild form of carrot. The carrots on the right have been improved over hundreds of years by farmers.

v v A mule is a cross between two closely related species, a donkey and a horse. Mules cannot run as fast as horses but they can run for longer.

Breeding healthier animals and plants takes a long time and the results are not always what you expect.

Genetically engineering a new plant or animal is faster and more easily controlled. Scientists can choose just one gene that codes for a particular characteristic and "switch" it off or transfer it to another living thing. Plant and animal genes can be transferred to different plants and animals.

When a living thing has a gene from another species of animal or plant we call it a **transgenic** living thing (*trans* means "across," so *transgenic* means "across gene").

Inserting the gene you want into another **organism** is the hard part. The piece of DNA has to be inserted into a single cell. The DNA must bind to the chromosome and then the cell has to **reproduce** to make a fully grown new organism. All the cells in the new organism will have identical DNA, including the inserted gene.

Who owns GM plants and animals?

Before you can transfer a gene from one organism to another, you have to find it among the rest of the complicated genetic code. It is then decoded. The bit of DNA you want is cut and inserted into the DNA of the other organism.

This process can take many years of scientific research. Companies experimenting with genetic modification spend a lot of money on research. Once they have successfully produced a GM plant or animal, they hope to get their money back by selling their product.

Companies often obtain a **patent** for the gene they have decoded and the new genetically modified organism containing that gene.

∧ Patent documents explain the invention
∧ or discovery that has been patented
and identify its owner.

Patents

Patents are legal documents that state who owns the science, technology, or design behind an invention or discovery. Only the owner of a patent can use the invention or discovery or sell it to other people to use.

Some companies decide to patent a decoded gene as well as the GM plants containing the gene. They can also insert another gene so that the seeds from the plants are **infertile**. This means that farmers cannot plant the seeds to produce a new crop of plants. The farmers have to buy new seed from the company every season.

Modifying non-food crops

Non-food crops are plants that we do not usually eat, such as carnations or cotton. Genetic engineering can be used to make new colors in flowers or to produce plants that are resistant to insects and poisons.

Blue carnations

Carnations are very popular flowers. Carnation growers have never been able to breed purple or blue carnations. A company in Australia has genetically modified carnations by taking a gene from a petunia, a plant that naturally produces blue flowers, and putting it into carnations. They have also "switched off" another gene so that the carnations stay fresh in a vase for much longer.

1 Color genes are taken from petunia flowers and put into tiny living things called bacteria.

Bacteria

2 Bacteria are able to put petunia genes into carnations.

3 Carnation shoots are produced and plants are grown in a greenhouse.

^ Genetically modified carnations contain a blue gene from petunias.

Insect resistant cotton

Cotton grows on bushes. The fibers that are used to make cotton thread and cloth are the seed hairs from the cotton plant. Cotton plants get attacked by an insect pest called the cotton boll weevil. It burrows into the seed pod and destroys the cotton. A **bacterium** called Bt produces a chemical that poisons cotton boll weevils. The gene that codes for this poison has been transferred into cotton plants so that they are no longer attacked by the weevils. The farmers now use much less insect spray on their crops. This saves money and reduces the amount of insect spray in the environment.

Should we produce GM non-food crops?

Many people believe that genetically modifying non-food crops is acceptable. They are only worried about foods. Other people are worried that the modifications might somehow get into other organisms. One worry with the cotton plants is that the poison they produce to kill the boll weevils might kill helpful insects such as bees. Some people think it is wasteful to spend so much time and money making GM plants such as blue flowers.

GM food crops

GM soy

Soy milk and bean curd are made from beans of the soy plant. Over half of the processed foods in the supermarket contain something made from soy!

When you grow soy, there is always a problem with weeds. Farmers usually use a specialized **herbicide** to kill the weeds but not the soy. They have to spray carefully and at particular times to avoid damaging the soy.

^ All of these products contain soy.

One company has transferred a gene into soy so that it is resistant to a general herbicide called glyphosate. Glyphosate usually kills all plants. It cannot tell the difference between weeds and soy. It is quicker, cheaper, and less harmful to the environment than the specialized herbicide. If farmers spray their GM soy with glyphosate then the weeds die and the soy lives.

>>
Genetically modified soy plants are resistant to the herbicide glyphosate.

Genetic gossip

In 1994, the first GM food was licensed for human consumption—the FlavrSavr® tomato. An American company produced a tomato that could ripen without getting soft, so it tasted good and could be stored without being squashed. The tomato was changed. The gene that coded for the substance that makes tomatoes go soft was "switched off."

Some people think that pollen from the GM soy may fertilize other plants. The glyphosate resistance gene could "escape." It could get into weed plants and make them resistant to the glyphosate. A strain of "super weeds" could develop.

Living factories

Another type of genetic modification uses living things to produce materials or medicines for us to use.

Silk milk

The silk in spiders' webs is stronger and more flexible than steel. Scientists in Canada are experimenting with transferring the gene for spider silk into goats. The goats will not be spinning webs; instead, they will produce unlimited amounts of spider silk in their milk. The "silk milk" will be used to produce a material called biosteel. Biosteel will be very strong and light and could be used in aircraft, racing cars, and bulletproof vests. It could also be used in medical science to make connective tissues, such as bones and tendons, for the body.

^ A spider's web is very strong and flexible.

Medical milk

Have you ever participated in the MS Readathon? It raises money for research into a disease called multiple sclerosis (MS). People with MS have faulty nerves which "short circuit." Normal nerves have a coating around them made of a protein called myelin. In people with MS the myelin coating is destroyed by their own bodies. Scientists in New Zealand are trying to put the gene that makes human myelin into cows. The cows will then produce milk containing human myelin. This could be purified and given to patients with MS. Hopefully their bodies will destroy the myelin medicine and stop destroying the myelin that coats their nerves.

>>
Nerve cells are coated with myelin sheaths.

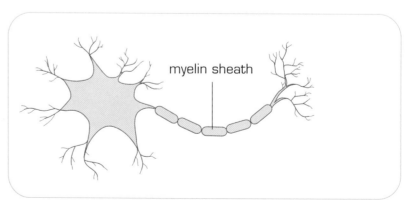

myelin sheath

The genetic modification debate

Genetic modification is a new and complex science. With genetic modification we can alter plants and animals in ways that were never imagined 20 years ago.

Arguments for

Some people believe that genetic modification of plants and animals will solve many of the world's problems because it can:

- ☑ make crops that resist ripening or wilting so they stay fresher for longer

- ☑ make plants resistant to pests and diseases so that we do not need to spray them

- ☑ make foods healthier by increasing the protein or vitamins, or reducing the saturated fat or sugar

- ☑ make medicines and other products. Using animals as "living factories" causes less environmental damage.

∨∨ Some people believe that GM non-food crops such as cotton are acceptable.

Arguments against

Other people are against any sort of genetic modification because they believe that:

- ☒ transferring genes between different organisms is unnatural

- ☒ transferred genes may escape and produce "super weeds" or other unwanted organisms

- ☒ GM foods have not been properly tested and may cause allergies

- ☒ large companies will use patents to control GM foods, and so not everyone will be able to benefit from them.

Other opinions

There are some people who believe that genetic modification is acceptable in some cases.

What is your opinion?

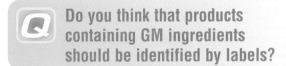
Q Do you think that products containing GM ingredients should be identified by labels?

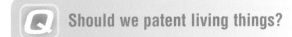
Q Should we patent living things?

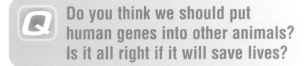
Q Do you think we should put human genes into other animals? Is it all right if it will save lives?

Cloning

Dolly the sheep

In 1997, Scottish scientists created a lamb using a cell from the udder of an adult sheep. The lamb was called Dolly.

The scientists actually needed three sheep to produce Dolly. The first sheep provided the udder cell. A second sheep provided an egg cell that had not been fertilized. The scientists sucked the nucleus out of this cell, removing all of its DNA. The two cells were put next to each other and an electric pulse was used to join them together. The cells then started to divide to form an **embryo**—just like a fertilized egg would do inside a mother sheep. The embryo was put into a third sheep and she eventually gave birth to a lamb called Dolly.

Dolly was genetically identical to the first sheep who provided the udder cell. The first sheep was her "mother," but Dolly was also the first sheep's identical twin, even though she was born several years later.

The experiment to make Dolly was not easy. The scientists managed to get 277 cells to fuse together, but only 13 sheep got pregnant. Even then, only one lamb was born alive. Dolly became famous because she was the first mammal to be produced by this process, which is called cloning.

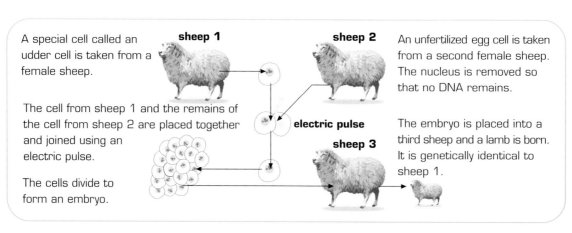

A special cell called an udder cell is taken from a female sheep.

sheep 1

sheep 2

An unfertilized egg cell is taken from a second female sheep. The nucleus is removed so that no DNA remains.

The cell from sheep 1 and the remains of the cell from sheep 2 are placed together and joined using an electric pulse.

electric pulse

sheep 3

The embryo is placed into a third sheep and a lamb is born. It is genetically identical to sheep 1.

The cells divide to form an embryo.

∧ This diagram shows how Dolly was cloned.

Cloning animals and plants

The process used to make Dolly was a type of cloning. A clone is an exact copy of another plant or animal. Identical twins are clones of each other.

Many plants reproduce by cloning. A spider plant grows clones of itself all the time. Gardeners grow new plants by cloning. If you take a cutting from a rose bush and plant it in the ground, you get a whole new rose bush identical to the first one. You have cloned the rose. You can do the same sort of thing with potatoes. You can cut the "eye" from a potato, put it in the ground, and a whole new potato plant will grow. It will be an exact copy of the parent plant that the potato came from. Even some simple animals such as tapeworms and aphids can reproduce by cloning. Genetic engineers can now clone mammals such as sheep, cattle, and mice.

∧ New spider plants can grow from the ends of special stems of the original plant.

What are the issues about cloning?

Cloning plants is not an issue. Many people believe that cloning animals is unnatural. We probably do not know enough about cloned animals yet. The possibility that we may one day be able to clone humans worries many people.

Q Do you think that cloning plants is acceptable?

Q Do you think it is all right to clone farm animals? What about humans?

Q Would it be all right to clone parts of a human (such as skin or nerves) to replace damaged or diseased parts?

<<
Should we ever clone humans?

How cloning works

Dolly the sheep was an amazing scientific breakthrough because, up until then, no one had ever taken a specialized cell and made a whole new animal from it.

We all start life as a single cell. That cell divides in two, then four, then eight, and so on. All these cells contain identical DNA and, at first, all the cells are identical. As we develop further, our cells begin to change into the type they will be when they are fully formed. Some become skin cells, others become liver cells, heart cells, and so on. The cells become **differentiated**. They do this by "switching off" some of their genes. A heart cell contains the information to be a liver cell or an eye cell but only the heart cell information stays "switched on."

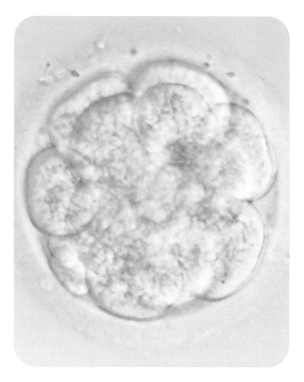

^ The cells in this embryo all look the same.

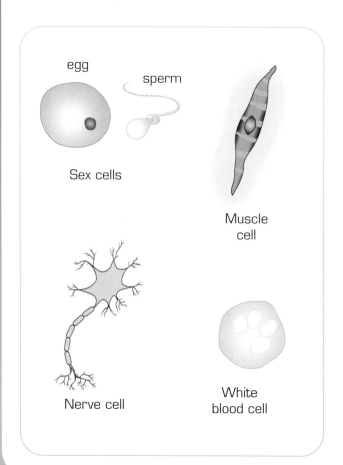

egg

sperm

Sex cells

Muscle cell

Nerve cell

White blood cell

Scientists thought that cell differentiation could not be reversed. For example, once a cell turned into a skin cell it could not change into another sort of cell. When Dolly was born, it was the first time scientists had taken a specialized cell (an udder cell) and turned it back into an undifferentiated cell. They had made the udder cell "switch" on all its genes again. It had been reprogrammed.

One problem with Dolly is that when she was born her cells were the same age as her mother's cells. This may be why she became ill and had to be put down at a young age.

<<
These cells look different from each other. They are specialized cells.

Cloning animals

Many of the animals that have been cloned are farm animals.

Australian scientists have inserted a gene into the DNA of cows so that they produce milk that is more **nutritious**. The scientists cloned the cows so that four identical GM animals were produced instead of only one.

One of the problems with cloning is that it reduces the amount of difference in a group. Usually, a herd of cows or a flock of sheep will have animals that are all genetically different. Some will be bigger or stronger than others. Some will have better wool or produce more milk. Some will be more resistant to diseases than others. So if a disease comes along, it might kill some animals but will probably not kill all of them. The disease resistant animals will survive and pass on their characteristics to their offspring.

A herd of cloned animals will all have exactly the same characteristics. They will be the same size and produce the same wool or milk. They will also have exactly the same resistance to disease. So if a disease comes along that kills one animal, it will probably kill all of them. No animals will survive to pass on their characteristics to the next generation.

> ∨∨ Cloned cows will produce high protein milk but they all have the same resistance to disease. A disease that kills one cow will kill every cow.

Cloning for "spare parts"

Many people have operations called transplants to replace internal organs such as hearts or kidneys. An unhealthy organ is removed and replaced with a healthier one from a person who has agreed to donate their organ. However, it is often difficult to find a donor. Even if a person receives a transplant, they have to take drugs so that their body does not reject the donated organ. In the future, cloning may be used to produce "spare parts" for humans.

Cloning organs

Cloning could overcome the rejection problem. If doctors could take a cell from a person who needs a kidney, and clone a new kidney, then there would be no rejection problem. The kidney would be compatible with the person because it is made from them.

Cloning of one organ does happen already. Skin can be cloned and it is used to repair the skin of people who have been badly burned. Usually, a piece of skin is taken from an unburned part of the body and **grafted** onto the damaged part. Sometimes, a person is so badly burned that there is not enough "good" skin left for grafting. Doctors can take a tiny piece of good skin and put it into a special solution. A tiny piece of skin can grow into a sheet of skin about 6 inches (15 cm) wide. This can then be used for the skin graft.

∨∨ This person's skin has been repaired with a skin graft.

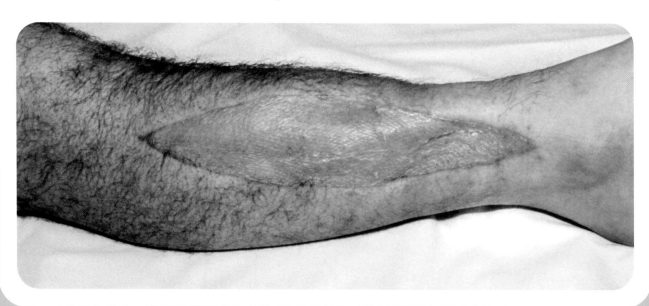

 # The cloning debate

Scientists have only recently worked out how to clone animals. It is difficult and the success rate is quite low. By working out how to clone farm animals like Dolly the sheep, scientists have discovered how to turn one sort of cell into another sort of cell and how to make a whole new animal from one cell of an identical animal.

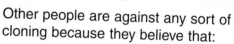 ## Arguments against

Other people are against any sort of cloning because they believe that:

- ☒ cloning is unnatural and goes against the laws of nature
- ☒ cloned animals (which are all identical) will all have the same resistance to diseases
- ☒ eventually it may lead to the cloning of humans.

 ## Arguments for

Some people believe that cloning is a great advance in science because:

- ☑ it will allow us to produce copies of farm animals and racehorses that have the best characteristics in the herd
- ☑ eventually it may lead to the cloning of humans
- ☑ it allows us to make human replacement body parts for transplants that will not be rejected.

Other opinions

There are some people who believe that cloning might be acceptable in some cases, especially if it helps to cure diseases.

What is your opinion?

Q If you had a disease that could be cured by a transplant, would you want to use an organ that was cloned from yourself?

Q Do you think parents should be able to clone their children?

<< Dolly the sheep was the world's first cloned mammal. Should cloning continue?

Summary

Genetic engineers are making new discoveries every day. They are finding out incredible details about who we are and how living things work. They can change living things in ways that were not thought possible a few years ago. In this book, some of the issues that surround genetic engineering have been raised.

ISSUE 1 DNA profiling

- DNA profiling can be used to identify individuals.
- DNA profiles are now used, as well as fingerprints, to solve crimes.
- Unlike a fingerprint, a DNA profile can reveal other sensitive information.

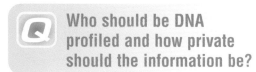 Who should be DNA profiled and how private should the information be?

ISSUE 2 Genetic modification

- Genetic modification allows scientists to change a single characteristic in a plant or an animal.
- GM crops are resistant to pests and diseases.
- GM animals can be used as living "factories."

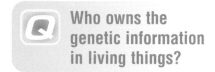 Who owns the genetic information in living things?

ISSUE 3 Cloning

- Cloning allows us to make exact copies of living things.
- GM sheep and cows have been cloned.
- Scientists are working on cloning body parts for transplants.

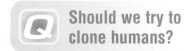 Should we try to clone humans?

THE FUTURE ▶

In the future, genetic engineers may be able to replace faulty DNA in people so that genetically inherited diseases could be cured. There are some reports that genetic engineers may also be able to take DNA from some extinct species and clone a whole new animal.

Glossary

bacterium	a type of microscopic living organism (When there is more than one they are called bacteria.)
cells	the building blocks that make up all living things
chromosomes	thread-like structures that are in the nucleus of all cells. They are made of DNA and contain your genes.
clone	to make an exact copy of another living thing
differentiated	having a structure suited to a particular function
DNA profiling	making a "bar code" of your DNA that can be used to identify you
dominant	stronger or more powerful. A dominant gene masks the effect of a recessive gene.
embryo	the form of an animal very early in its development
enzymes	chemicals in the human body
genes	parts of a chromosome that contain codes for certain proteins
genetic engineers	scientists who experiment with decoding and making changes to DNA
grafted	transplanted a piece of skin or other organ
helix	a spiral or screw shape
herbicide	a poison that kills plants
infertile	unable to reproduce
inherited	received genetic characteristics from parents
nucleus	the center of a cell
nutritious	containing things that are good for your health
organism	any living thing
patent	a legal document that says who owns the science, technology, or design behind an invention or discovery
pesticides	poisons that kills pests
proteins	substances making up your cells, and that control the activities in your body
recessive	weaker or less powerful. A recessive gene is masked by the effects of a dominant gene.
reproduce	produce a copy, have offspring (babies)
resistant	not affected by something
saliva	digestive juices in your mouth (spit)
transgenic	containing genes from a different type of living thing

Index